In Honor
of
All Veterans

U.S. WARS

THE MEXICAN-
AMERICAN WAR

A MyReportLinks.com Book

Kim A. O'Connell

MyReportLinks.com Books

 an imprint of
Enslow Publishers, Inc.
Box 398, 40 Industrial Road
Berkeley Heights, NJ 07922
USA

J973.62
OCO

MyReportLinks.com Books, an imprint of Enslow Publishers, Inc. MyReportLinks is a trademark of Enslow Publishers, Inc.

Library of Congress Cataloging-in-Publication Data

O'Connell, Kim A.
  The Mexican-American War / Kim A. O'Connell.
      p. cm. — (U.S. wars)
Summary: Discusses the major battles, military tactics, and famous figures of the Mexican-American War. Includes Internet links to related Web sites, source documents, and photographs.
Includes bibliographical references and index.
  ISBN 0-7660-5131-5
  1. Mexican War, 1846–1848—Juvenile literature. [1. Mexican War, 1846-1848.] I. Title. II. Series.
  E404.O28 2003
  973.6'2—dc21

                         2002153588

Printed in the United States of America

10 9 8 7 6 5 4 3 2 1

To Our Readers:
Through the purchase of this book, you and your library gain access to the Report Links that specifically back up this book.
The Publisher will provide access to the Report Links that back up this book and will keep these Report Links up to date on **www.myreportlinks.com** for three years from the book's first publication date.
We have done our best to make sure all Internet addresses in this book were active and appropriate when we went to press. However, the author and the Publisher have no control over, and assume no liability for, the material available on those Internet sites or on other Web sites they may link to.
The usage of the MyReportLinks.com Books Web site is subject to the terms and conditions stated on the Usage Policy Statement on **www.myreportlinks.com**.
A password may be required to access the Report Links that back up this book. The password is found on the bottom of page 4 of this book.
Any comments or suggestions can be sent by e-mail to comments@myreportlinks.com or to the address on the back cover.

Photo Credits: © Corel Corporation, p. 3; Aztec Club of 1847, p. 39; Descendants of Mexican War Veterans, pp. 12, 27, 31, 41; Douglas Southall Freeman's *Lee*, p. 33; Enslow Publishers, Inc., pp. 20, 44; Library of Congress, pp. 1, 18, 22, 23, 24, 28, 30, 38, 40, 42; MyReportLinks.com Books, p. 4; Naval Historical Center, p. 26; PBS, *The U.S.-Mexican War*, p. 36; PBS, *The West*, p. 15; The Alamo.org, p. 17.

Cover Photo: Courtesy of the National Museum of the U.S. Army.

Cover Description: *Remember Your Regiment!* by H. Charles McBarron.

Contents

MyReportLinks.com Books
Great Books, Great Links, Great for Research!

MyReportLinks.com Books present the information you need to learn about your report subject. In addition, they show you where to go on the Internet for more information. The pre-evaluated Report Links that back up this book are kept up to date on **www.myreportlinks.com**. With the purchase of a MyReportLinks.com Books title, you and your library gain access to the Report Links that specifically back up that book. The Report Links save hours of research time and link to dozens—even hundreds—of Web sites, source documents, and photos related to your report topic.

Please see "To Our Readers" on the Copyright page for important information about this book, the MyReportLinks.com Books Web site, and the Report Links that back up this book.

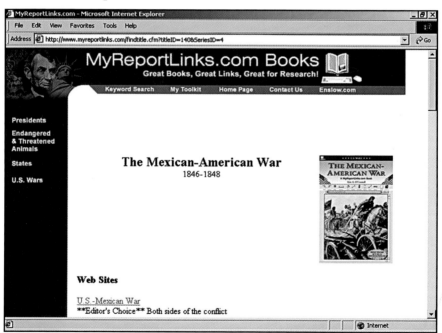

Access:

The Publisher will provide access to the Report Links that back up this book and will try to keep these Report Links up to date on our Web site for three years from the book's first publication date. Please enter **AMA3219** if asked for a password.

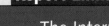

Report Links

➤ The Internet sites described below can be accessed at
http://www.myreportlinks.com

*EDITOR'S CHOICE

▶ **U.S.-Mexican War**
The Mexican-American War resulted in Mexico losing almost half of its
territory to the United States. In this bilingual PBS Web site, scholars,
historians, and authors share their views on the causes, effects, and
events of the Mexican-American War.

Link to this Internet site from http://www.myreportlinks.com

*EDITOR'S CHOICE

▶ **The Alamo**
This site features the story of the Alamo and its key figures, Davy
Crockett, Jim Bowie, William B. Travis, and Antonio López de Santa
Anna. A virtual tour and visitor information are included.

Link to this Internet site from http://www.myreportlinks.com

*EDITOR'S CHOICE

▶ *World Almanac for Kids Online:* **Mexican War**
The *World Almanac for Kids Online* Web site provides a brief overview
of the Mexican-American War, with biographies of the people involved,
including James K. Polk and Zachary Taylor.

Link to this Internet site from http://www.myreportlinks.com

*EDITOR'S CHOICE

▶ **The Battle of Buena Vista, February 23, 1847**
America's Story from America's Library, a Library of Congress Web site,
tells the story of the Battle of Buena Vista in which 5,000 American
soldiers turned back 14,000 Mexican soldiers.

Link to this Internet site from http://www.myreportlinks.com

*EDITOR'S CHOICE

▶ **Treaty of Guadalupe Hidalgo**
The Treaty of Guadalupe Hidalgo called for Mexico to cede 55 percent
of its territory in the United States. Here you will find the text of the
treaty, an article about its history, and related maps.

Link to this Internet site from http://www.myreportlinks.com

*EDITOR'S CHOICE

▶ **Welcome to the U.S.-Mexican War, 1846–1848**
This comprehensive site from the Descendants of Mexican War
Veterans contains images, maps, treaties, battle reports, statistics, a time
line, and links to related historic sites.

Link to this Internet site from http://www.myreportlinks.com

Report Links

 The Internet sites described below can be accessed at
http://www.myreportlinks.com

Adams-Onís Treaty of 1819
The Adams-Onís Treaty of 1819 was named for John Quincy Adams of the
United States and Louis de Onís of Spain. It renounced any claim of the
United States to Texas. It is also sometimes referred to as the Florida Treaty.
Here you will find the complete text of the agreement.

Link to this Internet site from http://www.myreportlinks.com

Antonio López de Santa Anna
Antonio López de Santa Anna was the dominant figure in Mexican politics for
much of the nineteenth century. Here you will find a brief overview of his life
and political and military career.

Link to this Internet site from http://www.myreportlinks.com

Aztec Club of 1847—Military Society of the Mexican War
The Aztec Club was founded in 1847 by American soldiers in Mexico City
who were veterans of the war. The society's membership included three United
States presidents. Here you will find the history of the organization and of the
Mexican-American War.

Link to this Internet site from http://www.myreportlinks.com

The Battle of San Jacinto
This Texas State Library and Archives Commission site is dedicated to the
Battle of San Jacinto. Here you will find background on the conflict, a
battle description, first-person accounts of the battle, and articles about
Santa Anna's surrender.

Link to this Internet site from http://www.myreportlinks.com

The Bear Flag Revolt and the Anglo-American Conquest of California
This page from the California Military Museum tells the story of the
Mexican-American War as it pertains to California. The Bear Flag Revolt
resulted in California's declaration of independence from Mexico.

Link to this Internet site from http://www.myreportlinks.com

The Border
At this PBS Web site you can explore the historical division between the
United States and its neighbor to the south, Mexico. An interactive time line
gives a history of the Mexican-American border. A morphing map illustrates
the changes in the border between the two nations.

Link to this Internet site from http://www.myreportlinks.com

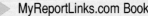
Report Links

 The Internet sites described below can be accessed at
http://www.myreportlinks.com

▶ **Captain Robert F. Stockton, USN (1795–1866)**
Captain Robert F. Stockton participated in the War of 1812, the
Mexican-American War, and the Civil War. This page from the
Department of the Navy Naval Historical Center site contains a
brief biography and several images.

Link to this Internet site from http://www.myreportlinks.com

▶ **Douglas Southall Freeman: R. E. Lee**
Here you will find the complete text of Douglas Southall Freeman's
comprehensive four-volume biography of Robert E. Lee. Chapters
twelve through seventeen document Lee's experiences in the Mexican-
American War.

Link to this Internet site from http://www.myreportlinks.com

▶ **The Gadsden Purchase Was Signed in Mexico City
December 30, 1853**
America's Story from America's Library, a Library of Congress Web site,
tells the story of the day that the United States bought approximately
29,000 square miles of land from Mexico for $10 million in the
Gadsden Purchase.   Link to this Internet site from http://www.myreportlinks.com

▶ **General Stephen Watts Kearny**
Stephen Kearny was a soldier, explorer, builder, writer, and statesman.
He fought in the War of 1812 and the Mexican-American War. Here
you will learn about his life and adventures.

Link to this Internet site from http://www.myreportlinks.com

▶ **Harpweek: John Charles Frémont**
John Charles Frémont was an explorer, writer, United States general,
and two-time presidential candidate. This biography contains
information about his life and adventures.

Link to this Internet site from http://www.myreportlinks.com

▶ **INVASIÓN YANQUI: The Mexican War**
Here you will find a history of the Mexican-American War and a
wide array of early photographs, maps, paintings, drawings, and
other images.

Link to this Internet site from http://www.myreportlinks.com

The Internet sites described below can be accessed at
http://www.myreportlinks.com

▶ **James Polk: The Manifest Destiny President**
This site provides a comprehensive biography of James K. Polk. Here you will
learn about his life before, during, and after his presidency. You will also learn
about his election, campaign, domestic and foreign policies, and his legacy.

Link to this Internet site from http://www.myreportlinks.com

▶ **Mariano Arista (1802–1855)**
In the Mexican-American War, General Mariano Arista was defeated by
Zachary Taylor at Palo Alto and at Resaca de la Palma. Arista later became
president of Mexico. Here you will find a short biography, photographs,
and list of links to other articles about him.

Link to this Internet site from http://www.myreportlinks.com

▶ **The Mexican-American War (1846–1848)**
This site from the Hillsdale College history department contains firsthand
accounts of the battles of the Mexican-American War, including the battles
of Monterrey, Palo Alto, Cerro Gordo, Buena Vista, and Mexico City.

Link to this Internet site from http://www.myreportlinks.com

▶ **Mexico para Ninos**
This site from the Presidency of the Republic of Mexico contains information
about the history, government, land, and people of Mexico. In the history
section you will learn about the Mexican revolutions, the Mexican-American
War, and other issues from a Mexican perspective.

Link to this Internet site from http://www.myreportlinks.com

▶ **National Park Service: Palo Alto Battlefield**
Palo Alto was the first battle of the Mexican-American War. Here you will
find information about the Palo Alto Battlefield National Historic Site.
Visitor information, battle history, and other park facts are included.

Link to this Internet site from http://www.myreportlinks.com

▶ **Sam Houston**
Sam Houston was the governor of two states, the president of the Republic of
Texas, a senator, a congressman, and a soldier. He was also instrumental in
gaining Texas's independence from Mexico. This page from PBS's *New
Perspectives on the West* contains his biography.

Link to this Internet site from http://www.myreportlinks.com

Report Links

The Internet sites described below can be accessed at
http://www.myreportlinks.com

▶ San Patricio Battalion
The San Patricio Battalion, or the Saint Patrick's Company, of the
Mexican Army was comprised of Irish-Catholic deserters from the
United States Army. Here you will learn about their role in the
Mexican-American War.

Link to this Internet site from http://www.myreportlinks.com

▶ Stephen Fuller Austin (1793–1836)
Stephen F. Austin helped thousands of people settle in what is now
the state of Texas. He was also responsible for helping Mexico run the
colony. This page from the PBS series *New Perspectives on the West* tells
his story.

Link to this Internet site from http://www.myreportlinks.com

▶ Ulysses S. Grant
This in-depth interactive PBS Web site contains a wealth of
information about Ulysses S. Grant. Here you will find biographies,
descriptions of events, an image gallery, a time line, Grant's memoirs,
and many more useful sources.

Link to this Internet site from http://www.myreportlinks.com

▶ Winfield Scott, 1786–1866
Winfield Scott was involved in the War of 1812, the Trail of Tears, the
Mexican-American War, and the Civil War. Here you will find the
story of his long and prolific career in the United States armed forces.

Link to this Internet site from http://www.myreportlinks.com

▶ Worth, William Jenkins
General William Worth served in the War of 1812, the Seminole Wars,
and the Mexican-American War. He achieved notoriety as the
commander of the troops that captured Chapultepec Castle. Here you
will find a brief biography.

Link to this Internet site from http://www.myreportlinks.com

▶ Zachary Taylor: The Warrior President
This site provides a comprehensive biography of Zachary Taylor's life
before, during, and after his presidency, including his service in the war
with Mexico.

Link to this Internet site from http://www.myreportlinks.com

Mexican-American War Facts

▶ **Time Period** 1846–1848

▶ **Combatants** United States of America; Republic of Mexico

▶ **Total Casualties**
> U.S. Department of Defense statistics show that
> 78,718 U.S. military personnel served.

> Americans: 13,283 dead
> (1,733 battle deaths; 11,550 disease deaths)
> Mexicans: unknown, but estimated to be much higher

A Brief Time Line

1844—*November:* James K. Polk elected president of the United States;
> supports Manifest Destiny.

1845—*July 4:* Texas votes to be annexed to the United States.
> —*November:* John Slidell fails to negotiate land deal with Mexico.

1846—*April 25:* Mexican soldiers ambush American troops in disputed
> territory north of the Rio Grande; war begins.
> —*May 8:* At Palo Alto, General Taylor's troops defeat General
> Arista's troops.
> —*May 9:* At Resaca de la Palma, Taylor and 2,300 troops crush
> Arista and 5,000 Mexican soldiers.
> —*May 13:* United States declares war against Mexico.
> —*July:* U.S. naval forces take Monterey and Yerba Buena, in
> California.
> —*August 18:* U.S. forces under Gen. Stephen Kearny capture Santa
> Fe without a shot.
> —*September 24:* Gen. Zachary Taylor captures Monterrey, Mexico.

1847—*February 24:* U.S. forces under Gen. Taylor capture Buena Vista,
> gaining control of northern Mexico.
> —*March 27:* Gen. Winfield Scott captures Veracruz.
> —*April 18:* Gen. Scott captures Cerro Gordo.
> —*August 20:* Gen. Scott captures Churubusco.
> —*September 13:* Gen. Quitman captures castle at Chapultepec.
> —*September 14:* U.S. forces enter Mexico City.

1848—*February 2:* United States and Mexico sign Treaty of Guadalupe
> Hidalgo, ending the Mexican-American War.
> —*July 4:* President Polk announces ratification of Treaty of
> Guadalupe Hidalgo.
> —*August 2:* Remaining U.S. troops leave Mexico.

Chapter 1 ▶

The Heroic Children

To the young men who were suddenly defending it, the castle no longer felt safe. Called Chapultepec, it had once been the palace of Aztec emperors named Montezuma, who had ruled hundreds of years before. By 1847, the castle was still one of the main fortresses guarding Mexico City, the capital of Mexico. It also housed Mexico's military academy, including about fifty cadets in their early teens. A normal day for the cadets included drills and studying within the castle's high walls.

But this was not a normal day. The United States and the Republic of Mexico had been waging a war over Texas and other territories for more than a year. U.S. soldiers had pushed their way westward from the Gulf of Mexico, hoping to capture Mexico City. With the capital in their control, the United States could settle the boundary between the two countries once and for all. Chapultepec was the only obstacle standing between the United States and victory. But the young military cadets, along with older Mexican soldiers, were prepared to fight in order to defend the castle and their country.

As the sun stretched above the horizon that morning, the U.S. Army pounded the castle walls with cannon fire. Although damaged, the fortress remained standing. The Americans decided that the only way to capture Chapultepec was to enter its walls and fight man to man. At first they were easily killed as they climbed ladders to scale the castle walls, but soon they had enough ladders up to beat back the defenders. The Mexicans began to feel

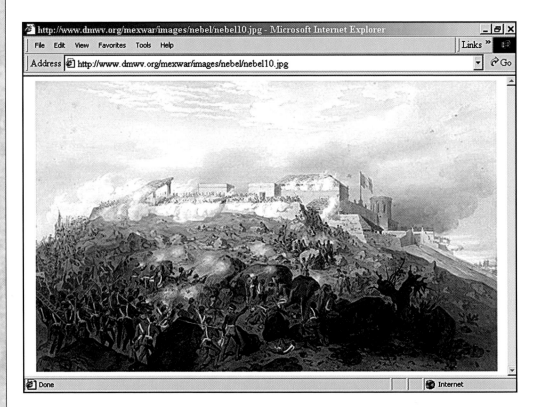

http://www.dmwv.org/mexwar/images/nebel/nebel10.jpg - Microsoft Internet Explorer

File   Edit   View   Favorites   Tools   Help   Links »

Address http://www.dmwv.org/mexwar/images/nebel/nebel10.jpg   Go

Done   Internet

The siege of Chapultepec, an ancient fortification that guarded Mexico City, was the last major battle of the Mexican-American War.

hopeless. They had called for reinforcements but they did not arrive. As the Americans raised their flag above the castle, many Mexicans surrendered.

But not all of them. According to legend, six of the young cadets chose to die rather than surrender to the U.S. Army. One of the boys grabbed a Mexican flag that had been torn from its mast. With the flag wrapped around him, the boy leaped to his death from the castle's high wall.

These six cadets are remembered as *Los Niños Héroes*—The Heroic Children—with a monument at the foot of Chapultepec. Their final act is one of the many episodes of bravery that took place in the conflict that became known as the Mexican-American War.

Although it lasted for only two years and has been overshadowed by the Civil War and other wars, the Mexican-American War is one of the most important events in American history. Up until the war, most of the land west of the United States belonged to Mexico. The war extended America's reach into the Southwest. It established the Rio Grande, the long river to the south of Texas, as part of the general boundary between the United States and Mexico. The United States acquired more than 500,000 square miles of land from Mexico, to help fulfill a policy to expand its borders from coast to coast.

Some people say the United States had no right to invade its neighbor to the south, Mexico. Ulysses S. Grant, long after he had served in the United States Army in Mexico and in the Civil War, called the Mexican-American War ". . . one of the most unjust [wars] ever waged by a stronger against a weaker nation."[1]

Chapter 2

The Forces of Destiny

In the early 1800s, the open countryside of Texas was mostly empty of people. Life there was rugged, but it was also free from much governmental control. Spain, which owned and controlled Mexico, had established the boundary with the United States through the Adam-Onís Treaty of 1819. Much of what is now the U.S. Southwest—Texas, New Mexico, and southern California—fell within the Mexican boundary. But with the capital far away in Mexico City, those few settlers in Texas often did as they pleased.

In 1821, Mexico won its independence from Spain. That same year, Mexico allowed Stephen F. Austin to start colonizing in Texas. Austin's father, Moses, originally had been given the right to establish a colony and bring 300 families to settle there. When Moses Austin died suddenly, Stephen completed his father's mission. Land was cheap and settlers, many of whom were slaveholders from the South, moved into Texas by the thousands. As they developed their communities and set up businesses, they became annoyed by some of the laws adopted in Mexico City. The capital just seemed so far away in both geography and culture.

Mexico was becoming alarmed by the freethinking colonists, too. The Mexican government passed the Law of April 6, 1830, preventing future immigration to Texas from the United States. The government also outlawed slavery. In addition, colonists had to pay large tariffs, which are fees placed on imported or exported goods.

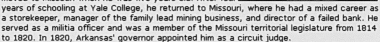

PBS - THE WEST - Stephen F. Austin - Microsoft Internet Explorer

File   Edit   View   Favorites   Tools   Help

Links »

Address http://www.pbs.org/weta/thewest/people/a_c/austin.htm   Go

PEOPLE

A-C
Austin, Stephen F.
Bent, William
Big Foot
Black Kettle
Brannan, Samuel
Brown, John
"Buffalo Bill"
Cabeza de Vaca,
Alvar Nuñez
Carson, Kit
Chivington, John M.
Chief Joseph
Clark, William
Clemens, Samuel
Cody, William F.
Coronado, Francisco
Cortina, Juan
Crazy Horse
Crocker, Charles
Crook, George
Cushing, Frank
Hamilton
Custer, George
Armstrong

D-H

I-R

Stephen Fuller Austin

(1793-1836)

Known as "The Father of Texas," Stephen F. Austin
established the first Anglo-American colony in the Tejas
province of Mexico and saw it grow into an independent
republic.

Austin was born in southwestern Virginia, but his family
moved to Missouri when he was five years old. After four
years of schooling at Yale College, he returned to Missouri, where he had a mixed career as
a storekeeper, manager of the family lead mining business, and director of a failed bank. He
served as a militia officer and was a member of the Missouri territorial legislature from 1814
to 1820. In 1820, Arkansas' governor appointed him as a circuit judge.

It was Austin's father, Moses Austin, who took the first steps toward establishing an
American colony in Mexican Tejas. In 1820, he traveled to San Antonio to petition for a
land grant, and in 1821 received approval to settle 300 American families on 200,000 acres.
But Moses Austin died before completing his plans and responsibility for establishing the
colony fell to Stephen.

Austin selected a site on the lower Colorado and Brazos rivers, and settled his colonists
there in January 1822. Almost at once he faced opposition from the newly independent
Mexican government, which refused to recognize his father's land grant since it had been
made under Spanish charter. Austin traveled to Mexico City to correct this situation, and
using skillful diplomacy secured a new law confirming his right to colonize the land and
designating him as the new colony's *empresario* or administrative authority.

Internet

▲ *Stephen F. Austin is known as the "Father of Texas" because he*
helped to establish the first American colony in what was then the
Mexican province of Tejas.

By March 1836, colonists had had enough. Texas declared
its independence.

▶ Uprising in San Antonio

Mexico would not let Texas go without a fight. Mexican
General Antonio López de Santa Anna and the Mexican
army traveled north to San Antonio to put down a rebel-
lion. Santa Anna, who was also the president of Mexico,
was enraged by the uprising in Texas. "I shall send four to
six thousand men to Texas with the purpose of punishing
those . . . North Americans," Santa Anna vowed. If the

Texans resisted, he said, he would take all their property and ". . . convert Texas into a desert."[1]

In early 1836, San Antonio was a dusty town that had grown around a mission, San Antonio de Valero, later known as the Alamo. By March, more than one hundred eighty Texans defended the Alamo that they converted into a fort. Colonel William Travis, a commander, knew that they could not last for long at the Alamo without help. He wrote to General Sam Houston, pleading for more men and supplies. But Travis ended his request like a devoted soldier: "Should we receive no reinforcements, I am determined to defend it to the last. . . ."[2]

▶ Remember the Alamo!

The siege of the Alamo began on February 23, 1836, and lasted for thirteen long days. On the still-dark morning of March 6, the Mexicans launched their final attack, pouring over the walls of the Alamo. By daybreak, all the defenders of the Alamo were dead. Only the lives of a few women and a slave were spared.

The Mexicans then turned their attention to the Texas forces at Goliad, a nearby town, where they executed hundreds of soldiers who had been prisoners. Instead of driving the Texans to surrender, however, the massacre increased their desire for independence. It also led Americans who lived in the East to awaken to the growing conflict in Texas.

The armies moved toward the San Jacinto River, and the Texans were ready for revenge. As General Houston led his fighters into battle, he urged them to "Remember the Alamo! Remember Goliad!" The Americans won the battle easily, killing almost seven hundred Mexicans. Santa Anna was held prisoner for several months and he agreed

 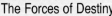
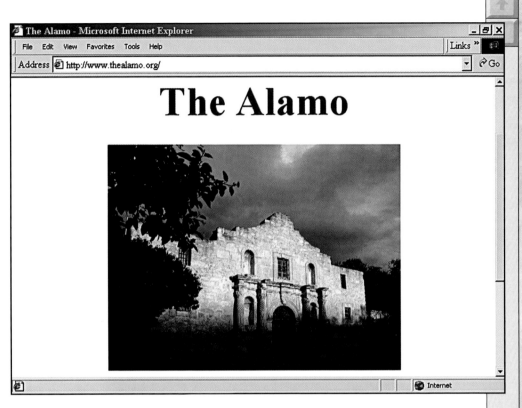

The Alamo

The Alamo - Microsoft Internet Explorer

File   Edit   View   Favorites   Tools   Help   Links »

Address http://www.thealamo.org/   Go

Internet

The siege at the San Antonio mission that became known as the Alamo brought Texas's fight for independence to national prominence. Cries of "Remember the Alamo!" would later become a rallying point for American soldiers in their war with Mexico.

to recognize Texas's independence to save his own life. He signed the Treaty of Velasco that made Texas an independent nation, but the Mexican Congress did not approve the treaty and refused to recognize Texas's independence.

Santa Anna remembered the Alamo and Goliad, too. He knew the conflict was just beginning. In 1841, he was elected president of Mexico, again. He had won glory in 1838 in a battle against France in which he lost part of his leg. Thereafter, he wore his artificial leg as a badge of

honor. Although he was replaced as president in 1845 by Jóse Joaquín de Herrera, Santa Anna's dealings with the Americans were far from over.

Manifest Destiny

In November 1844, the American people elected James K. Polk as the eleventh president. Polk felt that Texas should be annexed, or added, to the United States, even though it supported slavery. Many Americans, especially in the northern states, believed slavery was wrong and delayed admitting Texas to the Union. Texas had remained an independent republic for almost ten years.

Annexing Texas was just part of Polk's overall plan to expand the country. The American population was rapidly growing and moving west. Many Americans used the phrase "Manifest Destiny" to describe their feeling that they had a right to expand the nation. It was a powerful,

political force. Polk, who ran his campaign in support of Manifest Destiny, believed the nation should extend from the Atlantic Ocean to the Pacific Ocean. On July 4, 1845, Texas voted to be annexed to the United States.

President James K. Polk's desire to expand the United States led to the annexation of Texas in 1845 and an attempt to purchase the territories of California and New Mexico from Mexico. The latter failed, and the border between the two countries remained in dispute.

Mexico, however, would have none of this and broke off diplomatic relations with the United States. Complicating matters was the fact that Mexico still claimed the Nueces River to be the southern boundary between Texas and Mexico. Both Texas and the United States claimed the border should be about one hundred fifty miles south at the Rio Grande. That boundary added thousands of miles of land to Texas. Mexico refused to recognize the annexation of Texas or the Rio Grande border.

In November 1845, Polk sent a representative, John Slidell, to negotiate a land settlement and avoid war with Mexico. He was authorized to offer $25 million to Mexico to purchase the territories of California and New Mexico. In exchange, the United States wanted Mexico to recognize the Rio Grande as the southern boundary of Texas. The newly elected Mexican president refused to meet Slidell, and the talks broke down. The Mexican government and its people felt that this was a battle they could win. Both sides prepared for war.

Chapter 3

Crossing the Rio Grande— 1846

In January 1846, President Polk ordered General Zachary Taylor and about thirty-five hundred troops to advance south to the Rio Grande from their position on the Nueces River. He wanted U.S. troops to occupy the disputed territory between the two rivers. Taylor was a veteran of the wars with the Seminole tribe in Florida nearly a decade earlier. He had earned the nickname "Old Rough and Ready" because he was willing to suffer the same hardships on the battlefield as the troops serving under him.

The Mexicans protested and claimed this movement was an act of war. On April 25, Mexican soldiers crossed the Rio Grande and ambushed a unit of Taylor's men,

▲ A map showing Mexico's territory at the beginning of the war.

claiming the Americans were in Mexican territory because the Nueces River was their boundary. Eleven U.S. soldiers died in the skirmish. With this, the war had begun.

The front page of the Washington *Union* reported: "American blood has been shed on American soil!"[1] The loss of American lives gave an eager Congress a reason to declare war against Mexico, which it did on May 13, 1846.

In New York, a celebration in support of the war included new patriotic songs. One song reminded Americans of the reason to fight:

> The Mexicans are on our soil,
>
> In war they wish us to embroil;
>
> They've tried their best and worst to vex us
>
> By murdering our brave men in Texas.[2]

Other Americans were against the war. They believed the U.S. soldiers actually were on Mexican soil and that the U.S. government tricked Mexico into a war in order to win some of its land. Both sides had claims to the disputed territory.

Determined to take control over additional Mexican territory, the United States needed to accomplish several goals during the war. It had to make Mexico recognize the Rio Grande as the southern boundary, it needed to gain control over New Mexico and California, and it needed to capture Mexico City and force Mexico to surrender.

The Battles Begin

In early May, Taylor and his army were stationed at Fort Texas near the mouth of the Rio Grande. The U.S. Army was outfitted with fine uniforms. The infantry had dark blue coats, sky-blue trousers, and tall, decorated hats called shakos or casual caps. Varieties appeared in the uniforms

General Zachary Taylor earned the nickname "Old Rough and Ready" because of his toughness on the field and his willingness to endure the same hardships that those under him endured.

depending on rank and branch of service. By contrast, the Mexican army's uniforms were more colorful and ornate, with even greater variations than those found among the Americans.

To strengthen his army's position, Taylor had left a couple of regiments at Fort Texas and moved northeast toward Port Isabel on the Gulf of Mexico. Taylor's plan was to fortify Port Isabel, which he called Fort Polk, and transfer supplies from there back to Fort Texas. But on May 8, the Mexican army stood in Taylor's way. Mexican forces under General Mariano Arista had crossed the Rio Grande and caught Taylor's army between his two fortified positions.

Arista had chosen his position well. On one side of his army was a swamp and on the other a wooded hill. Taylor had no easy way to get around Arista, so he lined up his troops and waited for the firing to begin. Arista launched a volley of cannon fire, but it fell short of the Americans. Taylor was able to fire back and damage the Mexican line. All day, at a field they called Palo Alto, the two armies fired at each other. At day's end, Taylor claimed victory—only nine of his men had been killed compared to more than three hundred twenty Mexicans who had lost their lives.

The next morning, the armies met again near a dry riverbed called Resaca de la Palma. Although Arista had claimed good positions on the field, his army was spread out. Taylor sent his men into the riverbed to attack, where one small infantry battle followed another. Eventually, many in the Mexican army panicked, believing they were spread out too much to adequately defend themselves. Hundreds of Mexicans were killed, and hundreds more ran for their lives. General Arista left his tent so quickly that American soldiers obtained some of his writing paper and cheerfully wrote letters home on it.

Although the army rejoiced in these early victories, life was difficult in camp for both men and women. Wives of soldiers were allowed to stay with the army in the field, and several did. One woman, Sarah Borginnis, was nick-named the "Great Western," after a well-known steamship of the period. Borginnis was six feet tall and as strong as most men. Although she served as a laundress and cook to the army, she boasted that she could fight the whole

▲ *The Battle of Palo Alto, May 8, 1846. The United States troops under Zachary Taylor suffered only nine battle deaths compared to three hundred twenty Mexican soldiers who perished.*

Mexican army herself. Once, when an enemy shell exploded near enough to shatter a plate of food she was carrying, Borginnis still kept her wits and rushed to help the wounded.

▶ Conquering the West

With the hot summer upon them, Taylor planned to take the war into Mexico. As Taylor put his army on the march, other U.S. Army troops were also making advances into New Mexico and California. In 1846, the area known as New Mexico included the present-day states of New Mexico, Arizona, Utah, and Nevada, as well as parts of Colorado and Wyoming. New Mexico and California were the main prizes that Polk wanted by waging war against Mexico.

Colonel Stephen Kearny was ordered to gather volunteers and assemble the Army of the West, a force of about sixteen hundred men. In June, Kearny's army began its

▲ *The battle at the dry riverbed known as Resaca de la Palma resulted in another early victory for the Americans.*

march from Kansas to take control of the Santa Fe Trail, the main trading route to the West. By August, the Mexican governor of New Mexico had retreated at Kearny's approach. Americans captured the town of Santa Fe without firing a single shot. Kearny quickly took a few hundred men and moved on to California.

There, a soldier and engineer named John C. Frémont had been leading American soldiers in a revolt against Mexican control. Frémont proclaimed California's independence on July 4. Then, Frémont declared his support for Navy Commodore Robert Stockton, who had taken the towns of Monterey and Yerba Buena, which would one day be renamed San Francisco. Later in the year, Americans sealed their control over southern California with victories in towns near present-day Los Angeles.

Meeting at Monterrey, Mexico

That summer, Taylor's army had increased to fifteen thousand men, but soldiers were disappearing each day. Disease, lack of food and clean water, and the dusty terrain combined to make many soldiers flee for home. By September, Taylor marched with an army of little more than six thousand troops into the Mexican city of Monterrey. Monterrey was a strong city surrounded by mountains and man-made fortifications. It was the key to controlling northern Mexico.

There, General Pedro de Ampudia was waiting with a comparable force of more than seven thousand men who were backed up by ample artillery. Among them was a battalion of Irish immigrant soldiers who had deserted the U.S. Army. Called the San Patricio Battalion—or St. Patrick's Company—they were considered brave, fierce soldiers by Mexico but traitors by the United States.

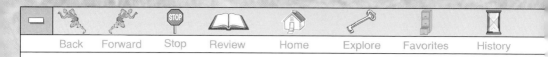
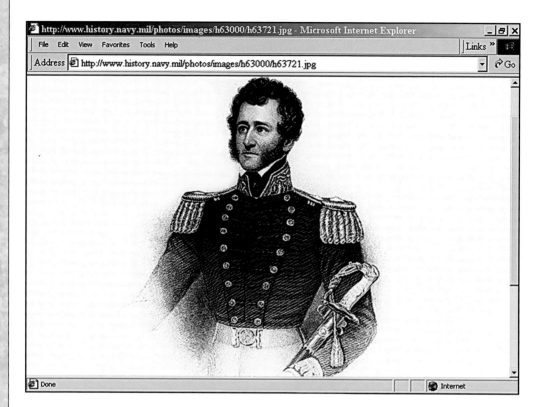

http://www.history.navy.mil/photos/images/h63000/h63721.jpg - Microsoft Internet Explorer

File   Edit   View   Favorites   Tools   Help   Links »

Address http://www.history.navy.mil/photos/images/h63000/h63721.jpg   ⬝Go

Done   Internet

▲ *Commodore Robert Stockton, a native of Princeton, New Jersey, had served during the War of 1812 and commanded naval forces in the Pacific. During the Mexican-American War, his victories at Monterey and Yerba Buena helped the United States take control of California.*

Taylor decided to divide his troops into two groups, sending a column of soldiers under General William Worth around the side of the Mexican army. Taylor would take a force against the front of the Mexican line. The attack began on September 20, 1846, and continued for four days. The Americans pushed the Mexicans into the heart of Monterrey, fighting from house to house. Taylor reported his losses as 120 killed and 368 wounded, but Ampudia's losses were greater. Monterrey citizens were eager for a cease-fire; Mexican women offered oranges to the invaders as a desperate peace offering.

Eventually, Ampudia offered to hand over the city if Taylor would allow the Mexican army to leave safely. Taylor agreed to the surrender. Back in Washington, however, President Polk was angry that Taylor had signed a truce without consulting him and let the enemy slip away. Tensions between the two men rose.

Although he was a tough soldier, Taylor was a just man. That autumn, he ordered his army to protect the rights of Mexican citizens. His soldiers still remembered what had happened at the Alamo, and some took their anger out on Mexican citizens by stealing property or committing violent acts. Eventually, two regiments of Texan soldiers were sent home. "With their departure we may look for a restoration of quiet and good order in Monterey [sic]," Taylor wrote.[3]

Monterrey had been a proving ground for several young officers, including Jefferson Davis, who would one day be the president of the Confederacy; future Confederate General Albert Sidney Johnston; and future Union generals Ulysses S. Grant and George Meade.

They soon would be tested again. In December, Santa Anna was reelected president of Mexico. He had spent the fall training his army to be stronger than ever.

Taylor's victories earned him the respect of his men and the admiration of the American public.

Chapter 4

Into the Heart of Mexico— Early 1847

In early 1847, California, New Mexico, and Texas were all under U.S. control, but Mexico was still willing to fight. To settle the land question once and for all, President Polk knew he had to beat the enemy on his own territory. This meant invading Mexico City "under the necessity of conquering a peace," as Polk liked to say.[1]

Polk weighed his options. If he ordered General Taylor to push south from Monterrey, it meant a long journey for the already battle-weary soldiers. Or he could put an army on the march from Veracruz, a port on the Gulf of Mexico. That army would then have a much shorter and direct route west to Mexico City.

But was Taylor the man for the job? He had become increasingly popular, and people back home were already saying that "Old Rough and Ready" would make a good president. Although Polk, who was a Democrat, did not seek re-election, he did not want to

General Winfield Scott was Polk's choice to lead the assault on Mexico City. This lithograph captures him in full military regalia.

give too much battlefield glory to Taylor, who was a Whig. Polk chose General Winfield Scott to lead the Mexico City campaign.

Like Taylor, Scott was a veteran of the U.S. Army, having served in the War of 1812. The soldier, who stood more than six feet tall, had earned the nickname "Old Fuss and Feathers" because of his love for dressing in full military uniform. Scott immediately wrote a letter to Taylor, requesting that he send a portion of his army. Scott could not resist a little boast. "Providence may defeat me," he wrote, referring to the mysteries of fate, "but I do not believe the Mexicans can."[2]

▶ A Difficult Victory: The Battle of Buena Vista

Unfortunately for the U.S. Army, fate did intervene. Scott had entrusted his letter to a young lieutenant to hand-deliver it to Taylor. Instead of going directly to Taylor with the instructions, the lieutenant stopped at a village to buy supplies. There, he was captured and executed. Scott's letter fell immediately into Santa Anna's hands. When he learned that Taylor's forces would soon be weakened, Santa Anna prepared for attack.

Scott and Taylor had figured that Santa Anna knew about the plans to land a force at Veracruz. They both thought that the bulk of Santa Anna's army would head there to resist an invasion. They were wrong. Taylor symbolized the enemy, and Santa Anna was interested in beating "Old Rough and Ready." Santa Anna's army was about fifteen thousand men; Taylor's army was down to less than five thousand men. On February 22, the unequal armies came together near the town of Buena Vista.

To even the score, Taylor positioned his soldiers in some of the area's best defensive locations on ridges and in

▲ *The Battle of Buena Vista was a costly victory for the United States and marked the end of Taylor's involvement in the war with Mexico.*

ravines. Santa Anna threw his army against Taylor's army in one attack after another. But the Americans were lucky. Whenever the American line was on the verge of breaking, reserve troops would come up or artillery would be put into place.

Despite the heavy assault by the Mexicans, the Americans held their ground. But they had sustained heavy losses, with about seven hundred fifty men killed, wounded, or missing. Santa Anna had lost about two thousand men. As the sun set on February 23, Taylor was not sure whether his army would have the strength for another day's fighting. All night, the campfires of the Mexican army burned in the distance, keeping the Americans nervous. Morning light showed that the fires had been a decoy. Santa Anna and his army had left the field.

Taylor turned to one of his fellow officers, John E. Wool, and hugged him in relief. The war in Mexico was over for him. Taylor was a beloved and faithful leader who had drawn cheers from his soldiers at Buena Vista. Now it was Winfield Scott's war.

Taking Veracruz

In early March, Winfield Scott and more than thirteen thousand of his troops were on board ships of the Navy fleet bound for Veracruz. For the first time in its history, the United States would launch an amphibious attack. As they neared Veracruz, the American soldiers found it exotic and beautiful, with its domed buildings rising above the city. But the fortress of San Juan de Ulúa in the harbor reminded them that this lovely city housed the enemy.

Landing at Veracruz required some of the newest military technology available, including small boats, called surfboats,

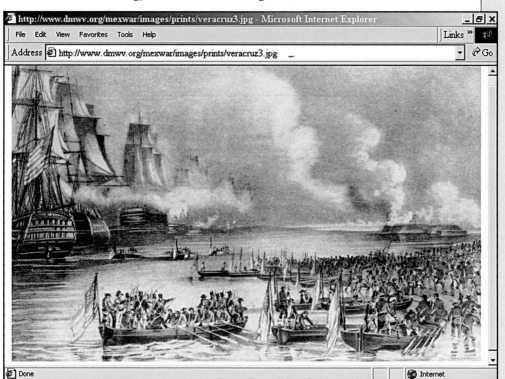

http://www.dmwv.org/mexwar/images/prints/veracruz3.jpg - Microsoft Internet Explorer

File Edit View Favorites Tools Help

Links »

Address http://www.dmwv.org/mexwar/images/prints/veracruz3.jpg

Go

Done   Internet

General Winfield Scott and his troops landing at Veracruz, March 9, 1847.

designed to transport soldiers from the larger ships to the shore. Although Scott had planned to protect the landing soldiers by bombarding the city with cannon fire, none was needed. The Mexican army did nothing as all thirteen thousand soldiers came ashore. Scott even had time to send his engineers—including a captain named Robert E. Lee—to design and build fortifications. Still, the Mexicans did not attack on a large scale.

On March 22, Scott demanded that Mexican commander Juan Morales surrender the city and the fort. When Morales refused, Scott responded by ordering his cannoneers to open fire. Shells bombarded the city for three straight days. Veracruz fell under U.S. control on March 27.

▶ Sneak Attack at Cerro Gordo

In April, Scott moved inland toward Mexico City. The main route, called the National Highway, was lined with mountains and hills. Santa Anna had rushed south from Buena Vista and had placed his troops on high ground around Cerro Gordo, a mountain pass. His soldiers lined up for two miles.

Scott had to figure out a way around the mountain. He dispatched Captain Robert E. Lee to scout the ground and find a solution. Lee pushed bravely as far as the rear of the Mexican line. At one point, Lee was so close to Mexican troops that he had to drop behind a log to conceal himself. Several Mexican officers even sat on the log to rest. Lee did not dare to move. Night fell before Lee, his muscles stiff and sore, could make his way back to his own army with information.

The risk had been worth it. Lee had found a route around the left side of the Mexican army. It required a lot

Robert E. Lee (by Freeman) — Vol. I Chap. 13 - Microsoft Internet Explorer

File   Edit   View   Favorites   Tools   Help   Links »

Address http://www.ukans.edu/history/index/europe/ancient_rome/E/Gazetteer/People/Robert_E_Lee/FREREL/1/1   Go

Done   Internet

Captain Robert E. Lee's scouting and strategies allowed Winfield Scott to achieve great victories at Cerro Gordo and Churubusco. Lee's distinguished military career would later prompt Abraham Lincoln to offer him the command of the Union army during the Civil War, a position that Lee did not accept.

of rough hacking through thick woods, but it likely would save soldiers' lives. An attack on the Mexican front would be too dangerous.

The next day, the army blazed a trail along Lee's route, pushing and lifting heavy artillery into position on Cerro Gordo, with a similar effort on a hill called Atalaya. Scott decided to fool Santa Anna into thinking his main attack would come on the right side of the Mexican army. He sent a small force to attack there. When the Mexicans were distracted, Scott sent the main body of his army to

attack on the left side and rear of the Mexicans, taking Santa Anna by complete surprise. With confusion all around them, Santa Anna and his army ran for their lives. Only sixty-four Americans were killed, compared to the thousands of Santa Anna's men who were killed or captured.

Scott was moved to tears by the bravery of his men. "Brother soldiers . . . your country will be proud to hear of your conduct this day," Scott told his men with his hat in his hand. "Our victory has cost us the lives of a number of brave men, but they died fighting for the honor of their country."[3]

Lee described the battle in less glorious terms. "You have no idea what a horrible sight a field of battle is," he said.[4] Yet for all its violence, Cerro Gordo had moments of kindness. Mexican surgeons on the battlefield helped the wounded whether they were Mexican or American.

Some Illinois soldiers could not resist having some fun. Santa Anna retreated so fast that he left behind one of his spare wooden legs, which the soldiers happily stole. Their souvenir was displayed in Chicago for many years.

Chapter 5

The Fight for Mexico City— Late 1847

After his embarrassing defeat at Cerro Gordo, General Santa Anna had no choice but to retreat to Mexico City. There, he agreed to send peace negotiators to meet with Nicholas P. Trist, who had been sent by President Polk to represent U.S. interests. Trist was an experienced diplomat who had studied law under Thomas Jefferson and was fluent in Spanish. Still, Polk did not entirely trust him. Polk became more anxious when he realized that it would take longer than expected to settle on a treaty. Santa Anna had agreed to negotiate only if he was promised bribe money. Bribery was not an option, so Santa Anna prepared his army for battle once again.

In those preparations, Santa Anna had help from the citizens of Mexico City. People melted church bells and other metal objects to cast new cannons. Muskets were purchased from foreign travelers. Residents opened their closets and trunks to turn over their own pistols. By August 1847, Santa Anna's army stood at about thirty-six thousand men. Scott's troops numbered almost ten thousand.

Although outnumbered, the Americans marched toward Mexico City, anticipating victory. At first sight of the great city, however, Scott and his men knew that capturing it would be difficult. Mexico City was protected on all sides by gates and other man-made fortifications. Nature helped, too; the city was surrounded by marshes. Because Scott was approaching from the east, that side of the city was the most heavily guarded.

Back   Forward   Stop   Review   Home   Explore   Favorites   History

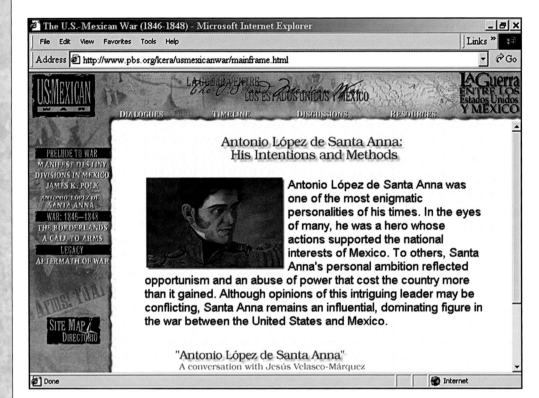

The U.S.-Mexican War (1846-1848) – Microsoft Internet Explorer

File   Edit   View   Favorites   Tools   Help   Links »

Address http://www.pbs.org/kera/usmexicanwar/mainframe.html   Go

DIALOGUES   TIMELINE   DISCUSSIONS   RESOURCES

PRELUDE TO WAR
MANIFEST DESTINY
DIVISIONS IN MEXICO
JAMES K. POLK
ANTONIO LOPEZ DE SANTA ANNA
WAR: 1846–1848
THE BORDERLANDS
A CALL TO ARMS
LEGACY
AFTERMATH OF WAR

SITE MAP
DIRECTORIO

Antonio López de Santa Anna: His Intentions and Methods

Antonio López de Santa Anna was one of the most enigmatic personalities of his times. In the eyes of many, he was a hero whose actions supported the national interests of Mexico. To others, Santa Anna's personal ambition reflected opportunism and an abuse of power that cost the country more than it gained. Although opinions of this intriguing leader may be conflicting, Santa Anna remains an influential, dominating figure in the war between the United States and Mexico.

"Antonio López de Santa Anna"
A conversation with Jesús Velasco-Márquez

Done   Internet

Mexico's General Antonio López de Santa Anna was a leader whose fortunes rose and fell as often as his allegiances changed.

Scott searched for an easier route. He again turned to Captain Robert E. Lee, who found a way around to the south of the city. Santa Anna eventually learned of Scott's movements, but by then the Americans had drawn nearer. In response, Santa Anna moved his base to a nearby town called Churubusco, located on the northern tip of a large lava bed called the Pedregal. Scott's men were stationed just south of it. They would have to get around that lava bed. Once again, Scott depended on Lee to figure it out.

Bloodshed at Churubusco

The route to the east of the lava bed was strongly defended, so Lee traveled around the west side of the

Pedregal. Accompanied by an infantry unit and some cavalrymen, Lee found a rough trail littered with molten rock. With some work, he thought it could be used to move troops and cannons.

With Lee supervising, a group of soldiers commanded by General Gideon Pillow opened the route around the Pedregal. But this plan was almost ruined when Pillow led a hasty attack on Mexican troops near the town of Contreras. The Mexicans came close to defeating Pillow until Scott sent reinforcements. Santa Anna and his troops then retreated to Mexico City.

Scott would have to get past the soldiers defending Churubusco, which sat along the Churubusco River, to get to Mexico City. There were two main ways to cross the river. One crossing was at the main Churubusco bridge. The other was at the fortified convent a few hundred yards away. Scott usually liked to take his army around or to the rear of the enemy. At Churubusco, he had no choice but to send the American soldiers across the main bridge. As the soldiers squeezed across, they were easy targets for the cannon fire.

Scott also sent his forces against the convent where San Patricio soldiers manned the cannons. They were the most determined defenders at Churubusco because they knew that if they were captured by the Americans, they could be sentenced to death.

After hours of bloody fighting, enough American troops crossed the Churubusco bridge to press the Mexicans back. The defenders at the convent surrendered and the battle was over. Casualties were high. Eighty-five San Patricios were captured and eventually fifty faced the death penalty. More than four thousand Mexicans were

This battle scene shows the pursuit of the Mexican army by the U.S. Dragoons at the Battle of Churubusco.

either killed or wounded—four times the number of American casualties.

▶ Last Stand at Chapultepec

Only one major obstacle remained in Mexico City: the Castle of Chapultepec. Chapultepec was the key to American victory.

Before he could take the castle, Scott sent a division under General William Worth to capture a group of buildings named Molino del Rey, which blocked the path to Chapultepec. Scott assumed that it would be an easy victory, but it proved to be a nightmare. Worth lost more men in one day than Taylor had lost in four days at Monterrey.

The Americans eventually conquered Molino del Rey, and Scott turned his attention to the castle. Scott's three top generals led the assault. On September 13, General John Quitman led the first advance toward Chapultepec from the south. Then, General Pillow attacked from the southwest and General Worth from farther west. Scott bombarded the castle at dawn, with the infantry assaults coming later that morning. Troops had to cross a heavily defended causeway, or land bridge, to reach the castle. Then they placed scaling ladders against the high walls of the castle to climb up and enter it.

Soldiers on both sides showed great courage. A lieutenant named Thomas J. Jackson attached cannons to two horses and drove them across the causeway. Before he reached the other side, one gun was disabled and another destroyed. But Jackson, who later would be nicknamed "Stonewall" during the Civil War, bravely stood his ground before he was backed up by more troops.

With ladders in place, infantry began to scramble up the castle's walls. The attackers included two soldiers named James Longstreet and George Pickett. Longstreet tried to storm the castle while carrying an American flag. When a bullet struck him, he almost dropped the flag, but Pickett

MEXICAN WAR -- Aztec Club of 1847 - Military Society of the Mexican War -- Union General Biogra -

File   Edit   View   Favorites   Tools   Help

Links »

Address http://www.aztecclub.com/   Go

Menu   AZTEC CLUB OF 1847   E-Mail

Internet

▲ *General John Quitman and his Marine battalion entering Mexico City. A famous account of the event notes that Quitman, later appointed governor of the occupied city, marched in wearing only one shoe.*

Ulysses S. Grant, whose lasting fame came during the Civil War, was first tested in battle during Monterrey. Here Grant is seen at the capture of Mexico City. Like Lee, Grant considered the price of American victories in Mexico too high.

quickly picked it up and carried it the rest of the way. They later served together in the Confederate army during the Civil War.

By 9:30 A.M., only the Mexican flag remained to be taken down, and the military cadets were its last defenders. With their defeat, Chapultepec fell under U.S. control. The conquering soldiers raised an American flag where the Mexican flag had flown. It was the signal that the United States had won. But it also meant that time had run out for the last San Patricio soldiers. They were hanged while the flag of their former country waved in the distance.

From Contreras to Chapultepec, ". . . the most astonishing victories have crowned the American arms," Ulysses Grant wrote to his wife. "But dearly have they paid for it."[1]

▷ Triumph in Mexico City

When American troops entered Mexico City, the fighting that broke out with angry citizens was among the bloodiest of the war. Santa Anna had even released convicts from jail so they could join the mobs attacking the Americans. But resistance vanished when the Americans began firing cannons in the streets. At last, Santa Anna surrendered with a note saying that the remnants of his army had left the city.

On September 14, 1847, Winfield Scott, in full-dress uniform, rode his horse into the center of Mexico City. Behind him was his victorious, cheering army. The army band struck up familiar tunes such as "Yankee Doodle" and "Hail to the Chief." Scott removed his hat and gave his army a bow.

"Veterans!" he called to them. "You have been baptized in fire and blood and have come out steel."[2]

http://www.dmwv.org/mexwar/images/prints/plaza.jpg - Microsoft Internet Explorer

File   Edit   View   Favorites   Tools   Help   Links

Address   http://www.dmwv.org/mexwar/images/prints/plaza.jpg   Go

THE OCCUPATION OF THE CAPITOL OF MEXICO, BY THE AMERICAN ARMY.

Done   Internet

This painting captures Winfield Scott's triumphal ride into Mexico City accompanied by the American army, which would occupy the city until the Treaty of Guadalupe Hidalgo was ratified, in August 1848.

Chapter 6

"Conquering a Peace"

In the fall of 1847, Nicholas Trist began to draft the terms of the peace treaty. As the weeks dragged into months, President Polk became increasingly worried that Trist would be too easy on Mexico when drafting the treaty. Trist ignored the president's concerns. Unlike Polk, he was there in Mexico City, and he knew that an agreement was near.

By February 1848, relations between Winfield Scott and the Mexican government had become friendly. Scott had been a guest at a festive dinner hosted by Mexican officials. Delegates from both nations agreed to meet on February 2 at Guadalupe Hidalgo, a sacred shrine near Mexico City, to sign the peace treaty.

Both governments had ratified, or approved, the Treaty of Guadalupe Hidalgo by May. The treaty recognized the Rio Grande as the border between the United States and Mexico. It also accepted the U.S. acquisition of the California and New Mexico territories—more than 500,000 square miles of

◀ Nicolas Trist was chosen by Polk to draft the terms of the Treaty of Guadalupe Hidalgo, which ended the Mexican-American War.

land. In return, the U.S. government paid Mexico $15 million for this land, known as the Mexican Cession, and more than $3 million to cover debts owed to Mexico by American citizens. The land in California turned out to be more valuable than anyone had expected. A few days before the peace treaty was signed, gold had been discovered in California's Sacramento Valley.

Money and territory could not make up for the loss of life. The Americans had suffered 13,283 dead, mostly to disease. Thousands more were wounded or had deserted. Because of inadequate records, the number of Mexican casualties is unknown but is estimated to be greater than American losses.

In November 1848, Zachary Taylor was elected president of the United States. He was so popular that he did not even have to campaign. Scott remained general in chief of the U.S. Army until late 1861.

▶ Growing Divisions

After years of struggle, the question of Texas was finally settled. But annexing Texas in 1846 as a slave state added to a growing dispute. People in the North and South disagreed about whether the remaining territories, when they became states, should allow slavery. The Compromise of 1850 allowed California to be admitted as a free state—maintaining the balance in Congress between the number of states that permitted slavery and states that outlawed it—but the debate was gaining steam.

Although he had lost the war, Santa Anna managed to remain powerful, as he had been his entire political life. He was even reelected president of Mexico and served from 1853 to 1855. During his term, Santa Anna worked with the U.S. government on the Gadsden Purchase, which redefined the boundary of present-day Arizona and New Mexico below the Gila River. But his cooperation with the United States angered most Mexicans, who in 1855 overthrew and exiled him. To them, the United States was still the enemy. Tensions between the two countries continued for generations.

▶ The Lessons of the War

Some historians argue that Mexico lost the war because its leaders lacked the patriotic spirit that motivated the Americans in their policy of Manifest Destiny. Many of Mexico's leaders, particularly Santa Anna, used the war to add to their own power instead of thinking about how it would affect the lives of their citizens.

After the war, the Mexican people began to develop a greater sense of national pride. Each September 13, the anniversary of the fall of Chapultepec, people gather at the monument to Los Niños Héroes, an enduring symbol of honor and courage. In 1947, on the one-hundredth anniversary of the battle, U.S. President Harry Truman

▲ The area ceded by Mexico to the United States in the Treaty of Guadalupe Hidalgo is known as the Mexican Cession.

laid a wreath at Chapultepec. Many say Truman's gesture began a new period of friendship between the two nations.

The battle of Chapultepec also gave the United States the opening line of one of its most patriotic songs, "The Marines' Hymn." This famous song begins, "From the Halls of Montezuma, to the shores of Tripoli, we fight our country's battles on the land as on the sea."[1]

The Mexican-American War was remarkable for a number of "firsts" for the United States. This was the first war fought outside the United States on foreign soil. It was the first war that used an amphibious invasion. It was the first war to be photographed. It was the first war that used newspaper war correspondents.

For Americans, the war proved the value of military education. It was the first war in which graduates of the United States Military Academy at West Point fought. In every battle, the Mexican army had more troops, more guns, and more cavalry than its American counterpart. Yet the Americans won every time, with far fewer losses. "I give it as my fixed opinion," Winfield Scott said later, "that but for our graduated cadets the war between the United States and Mexico might, and probably would, have lasted some four or five years. . . ."[2]

Less than two decades after the war, all that American military talent would be used again, but the enemy would not be a foreign nation. In 1861, many of the soldiers who had fought side by side in Mexico—Robert E. Lee, Ulysses S. Grant, Thomas "Stonewall" Jackson, Jefferson Davis, George Pickett, and others—would fight against one another in the Civil War. The question of extending slavery would be answered once and for all. If the Mexican-American War made the United States a much larger nation, the Civil War would make it free from slavery.

Chapter Notes

Chapter 1. The Heroic Children

1. Jean Edward Smith, *Grant* (New York: Simon & Schuster, 2001), p. 35.

Chapter 2. The Forces of Destiny

1. Randy Roberts and James S. Olson, *A Line in the Sand: The Alamo in Blood and Memory* (New York: The Free Press, 2001), p. 60.

2. Ibid., p. 117.

Chapter 3. Crossing the Rio Grande—1846

1. John S. D. Eisenhower, *So Far From God: The U.S. War With Mexico 1846–1848* (New York: Anchor Books, 1989), p. 66.

2. Robert W. Johannsen, *To the Halls of the Montezumas: The Mexican War in the American Imagination* (New York: Oxford University Press, 1985), pp. 230–231.

3. K. Jack Bauer, *The Mexican War: 1846–1848* (Lincoln and London: University of Nebraska Press, 1974), p. 102.

Chapter 4. Into the Heart of Mexico—Early 1847

1. John S. D. Eisenhower, *So Far From God: The U.S. War With Mexico 1846–1848* (New York: Anchor Books, 1989), p. 167.

2. Ibid., p. 173.

3. John S. D. Eisenhower, *Agent of Destiny: The Life and Times of General Winfield Scott* (New York: The Free Press, 1997), p. 257.

4. Richard Harwell, *Lee* (An abridgement in one volume) (New York: Collier Books, 1991), p. 62.

Chapter 5. The Fight for Mexico City—Late 1847

1. Jean Edward Smith, *Grant* (New York: Simon & Schuster, 2001), p. 69.

2. John C. Waugh, *The Class of 1846: From West Point to Appomattox: Stonewall Jackson, George McClellan and Their Brothers* (New York: Warner Books, 1994), p. 124.

Chapter 6. "Conquering a Peace"

1. United States Marine Corps History and Museums Division, *Customs and Traditions: Marines' Hymn.* <http://hqinet001.hqmc.usmc.mil/HD/Historical/Customes_Traditions/Marines_Hymn.htm> (n.d.).

2. John C. Waugh, *The Class of 1846: From West Point to Appomattox: Stonewall Jackson, George McClellan and Their Brothers* (New York: Warner Books, 1994), p. 128.

Further Reading

Carey, Jr., Charles W. *The Mexican War: "Mr. Polk's War."* Berkeley Heights, N.J.: Enslow Publishers, Inc., 2002.

Collier, Christopher, and James Lincoln Collier. *Hispanic America, Texas, and the Mexican War: 1835–1850.* Tarrytown, N.Y.: Marshall Cavendish Corp., 1999.

Garland, Sherry. *Voices of the Alamo.* New York: Scholastic, Inc., 2000.

McDonald, Archie P. *Historic Texas: An Illustrated Chronicle of Texas History.* San Antonio: Historical Publishing Network, 1996.

Nardo, Don. *The Mexican-American War: America's Wars.* Farmington Hills, Mich.: Gale Group, 1999.

Waugh, John C. *The Class of 1846: From West Point to Appomattox: Stonewall Jackson, George McClellan and Their Brothers.* New York: Warner Books, 1994.